# SEVEN THINGS THAT GOD DESIRES FOR US

*by Dr. George S. Dillard III*
*Senior Minister of Peachtree City Christian Church*

PEACHTREE CITY
CHRISTIAN CHURCH

LifeCast

**LifeCast Publishing**
*a ministry of Peachtree City Christian Church*
500 Kedron Drive
Peachtree City, GA 30269
770 487-9711

www.PTCChristian.com

Written by Dr. George S. Dillard III
Senior Editor: Lynn Horton
Administrative Assistant: Theresa Howard
Associate Editor: Jeff Morgan
Creative Director: Joyce Revoir
Design and Layout: Trisha Adams

Printed in the United States of America.

10 Digit ISBN:  1-4392-4350-6
13 Digit EAN:  9781439243503

Visit www.booksurge.com to order additional copies.

*I dedicate this book, of course, to my King*
*but also to Dad and Mom who taught me to love Him,*
*and to my wife and children who make loving Him real.*

# FOREWORD

It has been such a pleasure and a privilege to be part of the production staff of Dr. George Dillard's book describing the seven things God most wants for us, His children. George is passionate about sharing Jesus with everyone he comes in contact with. Whether at the coffee shop, grocery store, gas station, on the beach; he is always on the lookout for those who don't yet know the Living God. And stand back; he's going to share the Gospel message with an excitement and enthusiasm that is contagious! George brings that same fresh urgency to this wonderful project, his first book. How like him to take a negative aspect, what to some might seem to be censure from God's own words, and reveal in it a truth about our Father's incredible love and grand wishes for His dear children. I know this book embodies much of what makes George such a caring, dynamic, and, yes, sometimes overwhelming minister to his congregation. I believe George sees his efforts through this book as a new part of his discipleship, one we are all called upon to perform: The Great Commission lived daily through contact with others and in every way possible. It is highly probable that the truth explored in the *Seven Things That God Desires for Us* will indeed reach "all the world, preaching the gospel to all creation."

I sincerely believe that you will be excited with the premises explored here. There are so many potential applications for the seven chapters and the questions after each which elicit thoughtful personal response. George understands the importance of the individual's need to share their new insights and their growth—this then is their opportunity to do so, whether simply alone with God, with family, or in a small group.

So, it would seem that Dr. Dillard has given all of us a handbook which fulfills the tenants of The Big Mission—helping us through the exploration of this text to build our relationship with God, to offer others a loving introduction to Jesus, and finally, to grow in our roles as disciples of Christ. It is this mission that drives our church and our dedicated minister. It is my hope that your life will be touched and your walk with God enhanced by the lessons he shares.


Sincerely,
Lynn Horton
*LifeCast Publishing/Senior Editor*
*Sister in Christ*

*The Dillard Family*

# INTRODUCTION

During our annual family sojourn to Florida the very first week that school was out, I sat on the beach watching my children play and thinking through my morning devotional. There have been many teachers in my life regarding my relationship with the Living God, and each teacher has taught me about a different aspect and perspective of that relationship. As I sat that morning watching in awe the wonder and amazement of His creation,

I was reminded once again that the greatest teacher concerning my relationship with Him as Father has been my children.

As I watched them play, I thought about the simple, vital things I tell them to stay away from and why. When the red flags are flying at the lifeguard's tower, I tell them to stay out of the surf—not because I don't want them to have any fun, but because I know how dangerous a rip current is. When my children run right up to the edge of a busy street and I shout "Stop!" it is not because I am mean. It is precisely because I love them and am able to comprehend and understand the danger of crossing a busy street that I say "Stop." When it comes to my children, my love runs deep, my protection is a given and my direction is aimed at what is best for them. Jesus once said, "If you, as incapable as you are, give to your children only what is best in your eyes, imagine then what is possible when it comes to us from our perfect Father who is in heaven" (Luke 11:11-13, author's paraphrase).

As I considered my love for my children and my hopes for their futures, I realized that the depth of my compassion and what I desired for them paled in comparison to what

God wants for His children. As I thought back to the passage in Proverbs that I had read that morning, the simplicity of what I had missed so many times before now overwhelmed me. The Scripture tells us of the seven things God hates, but why? As I thought about the truth of this Scripture, this part of God's Word from a father's perspective, I could see that these seven warnings from God our Father are not meant to weigh us down; no father who loves his children wants to do that. I believe that what God our Father wants is for us to run away from the things He hates, of course, but more importantly, He wants us to run towards something of great value. Think about it. God doesn't tell us to run just for the sake of running; He tells us to run with a purpose. I began to realize that if God so fervently wants us to stay away from something, then there is surely that which He would like for us to find good, wholesome, attractive.

So, on that day, sitting in the sun on the Gulf of Mexico, thinking about the things that I wanted for the three beautiful children I love so profoundly, I began to consider some of the things my Father and yours wants or desires for us. These "wants" and "desires" became a list that when viewed even more deeply, was a good starting point for the valuable desires God has for each of us. You see, I learned, long ago that if God wants us to move away from one thing there is an exact opposite that He wants us to move towards. I believe that these seven hateful things are not a list to be checked off; rather it is the Wisdom of our God and Father telling us to stay away, that these seven things will hurt and even destroy us. Yet, what I know more than anything else is that the Father who loves us enough to send His Son to save us is saying to us, "If you really want to live, if you really want to know what matters in life, listen to Me and your lives will be fuller."

Now when I look at these seven truths I don't see the negative that God wants us to avoid as much as I hear His heart saying, "Here are the truths that will bring real life, rich living, the abundant life that Jesus Himself said He was bringing." The seven truths that this book shares are simple and ones that you and I can easily grasp; they will help us move closer to the heart of God, be more like His Son, and share His love in our relationships with one another. Isn't that what life is really all about? Loving God and loving each other. Indeed, those two commandments are what Jesus tells us that every thought of God rests on, and they are the heart of *Seven Things That God Desires for Us*.

I sincerely hope you enjoy this book as much as I have enjoyed exploring and coming to understand these seven truths from the heart of our Father.

God bless.

George S. Dillard

# CONTENTS

Whenever I read God's Word, I know there is a deeper meaning. These Words are the Heart of God, the very Thoughts of God, the Breath of God—These are His Words of life. I invite you to explore and to discover the Seven Things That God Desires For Us.

*There are six things which the LORD hates, Yes, seven which are an abomination to Him: Haughty eyes, a lying tongue, And hands that shed innocent blood, A heart that devises wicked plans, Feet that run rapidly to evil, false witness who utters lies, And one who spreads strife among brothers.*

(PROVERBS 6:16-19)

# ONE

## A HUMBLE HEART

The author of Proverbs says in chapter 6, verse 16 that there are six things which God hates. As is typical in ancient Hebrew poetry, the second verse is intensified as the author basically says "not just six things but seven things!"

*We will never run home as hard as we need to run home and never fall helplessly into the Father's arms until we admit that we don't deserve to be there.*

Five of these seven sinful things are associated with the body parts that cause these sins (eyes, tongue, hands, heart, and feet). It appears as if the author is purposely moving down the body (from eyes to feet). Not only is there intensification from "six things" to "seven things," but there is also intensification in wording from "hates" to "abomination." This word in Hebrew is *tôʿēbā*, which is the strongest negative word in the entire Hebrew language. On the opposite side of the spectrum of "abominable" is "holiness." If there are things that God detests, there must be things which God desires that are the opposite of these hateful things. If there are things that are abominable, there must be a holy parallel.

The first thing that the author of Proverbs names as repugnant to God is "haughty eyes" (the literal Hebrew term is "high eyes"). Often times in Scripture, eyes serve as a tangible form of a person's inner emotions. They can express malice (Psalm 35:19), grief (Psalm 6:7), and desire (Proverbs 6:25). In Proverbs 6:17, they are the bodily form of haughtiness, arrogance, or pride.

God abhors the attitude we adopt when we think too much of ourselves and consider ourselves better than others. Why is it that God hates haughtiness so much? The medieval theologian Thomas Aquinas concluded that "it is evident that man's first sin was pride."[1] Therefore, pride is the source of all sin. In the Garden of Eden, God told Adam and Eve,

> *From any tree of the garden you may eat freely; but from the tree of the knowledge of good and evil you shall not eat.*
>
> (GENESIS 2:16-17)

Yet, Adam and Eve seem to say or think, "God doesn't know what He is talking about; we know more than God." This arrogant attitude then leads to their rebellious conduct. Adam and Eve attempted to become definers of their own morality because they thought they knew more than God.

The opposite of "haughty eyes" is a humble heart. What exactly would a person characterized by humility look like? All too often a humble life is associated with a quiet, reserved, and withdrawn disposition. And although Scripture describes Jesus as the ultimate embodiment of humility, He was hardly a quiet, reserved or withdrawn person. The Apostle Paul said that Jesus

> *emptied Himself, taking on the form of a bondservant and being made in the likeness of men.*

> *Being found in appearance as a man, He humbled*
> *Himself by becoming obedient to the point of death,*
> *even death on the cross.*
>
> (PHILIPPIANS 2:7-8)

Consider the time when Jesus drove the money changers out of the temple. The Gospel of John tells us that Jesus made a

> *scourge of cords, and drove them all out of the temple;*
> *and He poured out the coins of the money changers*
> *and overturned their tables.*
>
> (JOHN 2:15)

Or consider the time when Jesus confronted the religious leaders of His day and said,

> *Woe to you, scribes and Pharisees, hypocrites! For*
> *you are like whitewashed tombs which on the outside*
> *appear beautiful, but inside they are full of dead*
> *men's bones and all uncleanness.*
>
> (MATTHEW 23:27)

Or consider when He spoke to huge crowds, thousands of eager listeners (Matthew 14:13-21; 15:32-39). Would a quiet, reserved person be capable of such a thing?

24

So if humility is not about being quiet, reserved, and withdrawn, what is it then? Humility could simply be defined as having an honest perspective of what really matters in life. An excellent example of this is in Jesus' final hours when He is in the Garden of Gethsemane. In agony, sweating drops of blood, on His knees He prays to God,

> not My will, but Yours be done.
>
> (LUKE 22:42)

Jesus understood that God matters most in life, that He comes first, and that everything else falls in place behind God. Jesus exemplified absolute humility by taking the form of a servant and dying on the cross.

How then do we live a life of humility? A good starting point is recognizing that we are all sinners and fall short of the glory of God. In one of His parables Jesus says:

> Two men went up into the temple to pray, one a Pharisee and the other a tax collector. The Pharisee stood and was praying this to himself: "God, I thank You that I am not like other people:

*'ers, unjust, adulterers, or even like this tax*

*᠌. I fast twice a week; I pay tithes of all that I*

*ᵹet."*

*But the tax collector, standing some distance away, was even unwilling to lift up his eyes to heaven, but was beating his breast, saying, "God, be merciful to me, the sinner!"*

*I tell you, this man went to his house justified rather than the other; for everyone who exalts himself will be humbled, but he who humbles himself will be exalted.*

(LUKE 18:10-14)

We must recognize we are sinners. If we never confess that we are sinners, we will never need God. It is easy to think to oneself, "I'm not perfect, but at least I'm not as bad as...." However, this is the same arrogant attitude that Jesus condemns in this parable. The correct response is "God, be merciful to me, the sinner!"

In order to live a life of humility, we must admit that we are not worthy. One cannot embrace the gift of God without understanding that it is undeserved, that it is by grace we are redeemed. In the parable of the prodigal son, the son returns to his father saying,

> *Father, I have sinned against heaven and in your sight. I am no longer worthy to be called your son.*
>
> (LUKE 15:21)

We will never run home as hard as we need to run home and never fall helplessly into the Father's arms until we admit that we don't deserve to be there.

You must recognize your limitations. I believe on some level we all struggle with this concept. At my house, we have a sink in our washroom that doesn't get used very much. A few years ago my wife, Renee, and I decided to repaint the washroom. I decided to remove the sink so we could paint the entire room. When I put it back, the valves were leaking. Renee insisted that I call a plumber, but I refused, saying, "I can fix it." So, I put new valves on and the pipes began to leak. Then I put new pipes in, and the valves started to leak. Then I tried to use some tape that stops ALL leaks. Right. After this failed, I decided we would just put a bucket under the sink and empty it every few days. I failed to recognize my limitations. I should have called for help when I needed it most. If you don't know your limitations, you are not going to ask for help.

In the Scriptures we are given a view into the life of a man who still elicits strong feelings in the minds and hearts of people even today, the man David. In thinking of David's life, two events immediately come to mind—one in which he realized his limitations and from the very beginning called on the Living God for help, and the second where David didn't admit his limitations or his need for help until after he had damaged or ruined a number of lives including his own. When the boy David faced Goliath in the valley, he knew that there was no possible way for him to defeat this giant without totally relying on the Living God. David did just that. He put his life and his heart fully in the hands of God, and that day the boy did the impossible. The giant fell and the Philistines and all of Israel saw the power of the Living God first hand. Unfortunately the second event recounts David facing another giant, not a nine-foot tall warrior, but a giant of staggering proportions none the less. This second giant was the desire of David's flesh, the lust that consumes and destroys without regard to age, gender, status, or position—the lust of the flesh, the lust of the eyes, and the boastful pride of life.

This giant is far more furious and destructive than Goliath, but David believed he could face and conquer it on his own; the results were disastrous and led to terrible consequences including the death of a valuable and trusted friend. Each of us must recognize that everyday we will face giants; and if we attempt to tackle them on our own, they will doom us to losing the battle. We must acknowledge our limitations.

After acknowledging our limitations, after realizing that we are broken and imperfect, we must acknowledge that holiness comes from God alone and righteousness comes from surrender. Righteousness comes from faith in God. It's not about following a system of rules and regulations; it's about surrendering to God. We must understand this in order to become truly humble. We must understand that we've sinned, we're unworthy, we have limitations, that God alone is holy, and that righteousness comes from surrender.

God desires humility for us so that we can identify and understand what really matters in life. Jesus once said,

*Seek first His kingdom and His righteousness, and all*
*these things will be added to you.*

(MATTHEW 6:33)

God promises to provide for our needs when we humble ourselves in His presence. Real humility allows us to be blessed because it demands turning our lives over to God and then letting Him be in control.

*Humble yourselves in the presence of the Lord, and*
*He will exalt you.*

(JAMES 4:10)

I have personally seen this displayed in the lives of many in my congregation.

Finally, God desires a humble life for us because our humility helps us see Jesus the Son of Man clearly. When we think too highly of ourselves, we let ourselves get in the way of surrender. When we look past ourselves, we can clearly see a man humbling Himself in front of an angry crowd and allowing Himself to be put to death on a cross by a hostile government. But this is not just any man. This is God Himself, in the flesh, humbling Himself to die for the sake of humanity.

# 1 CHAPTER ONE:  A HUMBLE HEART
# REVIEW

- What is the first thing God considers "an abomination" in Proverbs 6:16-19?

- What is the opposite of "haughty eyes"?

- According to the theologian Thomas Aquinas, what was the first sin?

- Humility means having an honest perspective on life and putting God before everything else. How did Jesus exemplify this in His life?

- We cannot accept the gift of grace from God without first doing what?

- How are blessings from God associated with living humbly?

# TWO

---

# HONESTY...
# SUCH A LONELY
# WORD?

---

The second thing that the author of Proverbs says that God hates is "a lying tongue" (Proverbs 6:17b). Certainly, the opposite of a lying tongue is the voice of truth. In 1978 Billy Joel

*People can often lie and cheat their way through jobs or school, but how are you going to fool God?*

wrote, "If you look for truthfulness, you might just as well be blind. Honesty is such a lonely word. Honesty is hardly ever heard."[2] Is honesty really such a lonely word?

Is integrity that hard to find in today's world?

We live in a time and culture where it is commonplace to believe that being honest is really not all that important and that, indeed, being "honest to a fault" is never a positive trait. How is it that as a society we could ever get to the place where honesty would be seen as somehow harmful, damaging or detrimental? Well, there is "truth" that is hard to hear, but I am certain that the absence of honesty is not what God wants from His children. Neither is the "white lie." It is true that often today many people see one who is "honest to a fault" as being obsessed with telling the truth, or even "just plain rude." Obviously, a "white lie" and being "honest to a fault" are not the same two things. An unspoken truth, like withholding a comment on your friend's terrible hairdo or awful tie is not a lie. However, telling that friend her hair or his tie looks great when it does not is one. A white lie is a lie, being honest to a fault is someone who is brutally honest and is not speaking in love. I always tell my children "You must tell the truth, but you don't have to tell everything you know."

The word honesty is not lonely; in fact, we toss it around all the time. "Honestly?" "Honest to Pete?" "Honest to goodness!" "Are you being honest with me?" All the time people are constantly begging one another to tell them the truth or to confirm that what they say is true. That is what lends the element of loneliness to the word "honesty." It is more the pity that we have reached the place in our relationships where we don't trust that anyone is honest with us; because honesty and integrity are traits that are no longer cultivated, no longer admired, and no longer esteemed!

In 1997 Jim Carrey starred in the movie *Liar Liar*. Carrey plays Fletcher Reede, a lawyer who has made lying a lifestyle. When Fletcher lies to his son Max and skips his birthday party, Max wishes that his father will not be able to lie any more. His wish comes true and Fletcher becomes totally incapable of lying. Fletcher implores his son to reverse the wish. He explains to Max at one point, "I have to lie. Everybody lies." Max then says, "But you're the only one that makes me feel bad."[3]

We live in a culture that struggles with honesty. We often don't stop to think of the effect that our dishonesty has on others. Jim Carrey's character believes that people have to lie to keep a job, to have a strong relationship, and to maintain friendships. According to a survey of the academically top 5% of high school students by the publisher of *Who's Who Among American High School Students*, "80% of the students cheated [and] 95% of those who cheated avoided being caught."[4] Do not assume that it is just teenagers who are lying. Many Americans "fudge," a nicer word than "lie," on their income taxes. "White lies" are considered acceptable. "Fish stories," which are embellished stories or tall tales, are common. Lying is epidemic in our culture.

It was once said that "you can tell a great lie if 80% of it is the truth." God doesn't desire "part of the truth" or "most of the truth" from us. God desires honesty through and through. God desires His people to be a sincere, genuine, loving community. Paul speaks about how Christians should be *"speaking the truth in love"* (Ephesians 4:15) as we continue to become more Christ-like. Dishonesty destroys any sense of fellowship within a community and causes pain to all those around us. Think of the boy's words in *Liar Liar*. Lies are destructive. Lies hurt people. Lies make people "feel bad."

The tongue is one of the smallest muscles in the body. However, this small muscle is capable of terrible destruction. For this reason, time and time again, Scripture warns us about controlling our tongue and the way we speak to one another. The majority of these references are found in the poetic and wisdom literature of the Bible—particularly in Job, Psalms, and Proverbs. Perhaps the most blatant warning of the necessity for taming the tongue is found in James.

> *So also the tongue is a small part of the body, and yet it boasts of great things. See how great a forest is set aflame by such a small fire! And the tongue is a fire, the very world of iniquity; the tongue is set among our members as that which defiles the entire body, and sets on fire the course of our life, and is set on fire by hell. For every species of beasts and birds, of reptiles and creatures of the sea, is tamed and has been tamed by the human race. But no one can tame the tongue; it is a restless evil and full of deadly poison*
>
> (JAMES 3:5-8)

If God desires for us to speak the truth, we must learn how to tame our tongues.

Often there is a fine line between speaking the truth and speaking the truth in love. Once again referring to *Liar Liar*, there is a scene where Max puts his dad to a test to see if he really cannot lie. Max says, "My teacher tells me beauty is on the inside," and Fletcher responds by saying, "That's just something ugly people say." That is not honesty, but brutality. One must find the balance. Truth must be spoken with love.

There are three things I want to propose in this chapter about why God desires for us to be honest. First, honesty is essential for having a fruitful relationship of any kind. Every relationship is built on trust. Without honesty, there can be no trust. Without trust, there can be no intimacy. This is not true just in romantic relationships, but in every type of relationship whether it is a relationship with a friend, a co-worker, or a family member.

Sometimes it takes years to build up trust, but only a second to destroy it. A few years ago a group of executives from a major German corporation were playing golf at the Stuttgart Golf Club, one of the finest golf clubs in the world.

There is a par three on the course that is a blind hole. The four executives teed off and seemed to make decent shots; however, when they got down to the green, there were only three balls on the putting surface. All of the executives looked for the missing ball. Then one of the executives, a young, eager Vice President, announced, "I found my ball!" Everybody stepped back while he chipped up onto the green. When the Chairman of the Board walked over to the flag to pull it out, he looked down into the hole and...there was the Vice President's ball. The young man had hit one of the most impossible shots in golf but never thought to look in the hole. So sure that he had lost his ball, he simply did what a number of golfers have done; he dropped a ball then claimed to have found the lost ball. Now as the Chairman prepared to remove the flag, he unhesitatingly announced, "You're dismissed." The message was clear; the ball in the cup spoke not of overcoming incredible odds, it simply said, "I lie." The Chairman believed that if the young man was going to lie about finding his ball in order to get one step ahead in a game, he could hardly be trusted in business. In that instant, he had destroyed all of his credibility by lying and, in disgrace, left the course and his career behind.

The second reason God desires for us to be honest is because it is essential in order to grow in faith. When a person reads the Bible and comes before God, he or she must honestly examine himself or herself. If we are not honest with ourselves, we will never understand our need for God. In Scripture, Satan is described as one who

> *prowls around like a roaring lion, seeking someone to devour.*
>
> (1 PETER 5:8B)

Satan does not attack your strengths, but your weaknesses. Therefore, we must be honest with ourselves and acknowledge our faults and weaknesses so that Satan cannot have an open season in our lives. When we honestly acknowledge our weaknesses, we recognize where we need God's strength the most.

Being honest does not affect just your "spiritual life" but your "physical life" as well. Though the physical element and spiritual element of a human are often talked about as two separate things, they are very closely intertwined and one greatly affects the other. If we are dishonest with "spiritual issues," this dishonesty can have physical ramifications.

For example, sexual immorality clearly is a sin and has spiritual ramifications, but it also has physical ramifications. It can lead to sexually transmitted diseases, the destruction of one's home or career, the loss of trust among family and friends, and in extreme situations the loss of life. Therefore, if we are honest, our truthfulness, sincerity and authenticity will benefit us in our spiritual lives as well as in our physical lives.

Honesty is essential for having a proper perspective on life. People can often lie and cheat their way through jobs or school, but how are you going to fool God? How are you going to bluff yourself? If we are unwilling to be honest with ourselves and recognize our own faults and sins, then we will never realize our need for God's grace. If we are not honest with ourselves we will never turn to God. Is honesty such a lonely word? Is it really that hard to find? It should not be.

# 2 CHAPTER TWO: HONESTY…SUCH A LONELY WORD?
## REVIEW

- What is the second thing God considers "an abomination" in Proverbs 6:16-19?

- What is the opposite of "a lying tongue"?

- What is the difference between speaking the truth and speaking the truth in love?

- How long does it take to build up trust?

- How long does it take to tear down trust?

- How does honesty or dishonesty relate to your faith?

# THREE

# AND JUSTICE FOR ALL

In the second half of Proverbs 6:17, the author moves down from the eyes and the lying tongue to the *"hands that shed innocent blood."* There is little, if anything, that God hates more than the loss of innocent lives because He is a

*What would these same prophets say if they walked into our worship services today? Are we attempting to worship God while ignoring the needs of the downtrodden?*

God of justice. Usually God's wrath becomes most evident in stories where there is blatant injustice. Consider the story of Cain and Abel. Cain grows jealous of the fact that God accepted Abel's sacrifice but God rejected his. In anger, Cain slays his brother. When God confronts the murderer about his crime, He says,

> *Now you are cursed from the ground, which has opened its mouth to receive your brother's blood from your hand. When you cultivate the ground, it will no longer yield its strength to you; you will be a vagrant and a wanderer on the earth.*
>
> (GENESIS 4:11-12)

After Noah and his family exited the ark, God put a ban on all unjust human bloodshed where man takes authority for justice. He said,

> *Whoever sheds man's blood, by man shall his blood be shed, for in the image of God He made man.*
>
> (GENESIS 9:6)

This ban, immediately following the exit from the ark, has led some scholars to believe that violence and murder were the vices that roused the fury of God to bring about the flood in the first place. God hates murder because humankind is made in His own image.

Consider God's amazing rescue of the Israelites from the bondage of slavery in Egypt. The entire nation of Israel was forced into slavery and there was state-sponsored genocide to reduce the number of Israelites. What was it that prompted God to act?

> And the sons of Israel sighed because of the bondage, and they cried out; and their cry for help because of their bondage rose up to God.
>
> (EXODUS 2:23B)

God heard their cry and miraculously delivered them from the bonds of injustice.

When reading the laws of ancient Israel, we must remember that they come upon the heels of the liberation from Egypt. Therefore, God constantly reminds Israel that they must treat outsiders with respect since they were once slaves in Egypt (Deuteronomy 24:17-18). The phrase *"Remember that you were slaves in Egypt"* is seen time and time again throughout the law. I believe that God cautioned the Israelites not to forget what it was like when they were slaves so that they would treat the people they encountered with justice; because they had been treated unjustly, they knew first hand how valuable fair and right treatment is. Israel forgot, as the church often does, that much of our purpose in the world is to show people who our God really is in the lives that we live, as well as in the words that we speak.

God is a God of justice. The absence of justice destroys our relationships with our fellow man. Perhaps this is the reason why the last six of the Ten Commandments are devoted to our relationship with other people:

1. I am the LORD your God (man to God).

2. You shall have no other gods before Me (man to God).

3. You shall not take the name of the LORD your God in vain (man to God).

4. Remember the Sabbath day, keep it holy (man to God).

5. Honor your father and mother (man to man).

6. You shall not murder (man to man).

7. You shall not commit adultery (man to man).

8. You shall not steal (man to man).

9. You shall not bear false witness (man to man).

10. You shall not covet (man to man).

This can also be seen in Jesus' teachings. When asked,

> *Teacher, which is the greatest commandment in the*
> *Law?*
>
> (MATTHEW 22:36 TNIV)

Jesus responded by saying,

> *Love the Lord your God with all your heart and with*
> *all your soul and with all your mind. This is the first*
> *and greatest commandment. And the second is like it:*
> *"Love your neighbor as yourself."*
>
> (MATTHEW 22:37-39 TNIV)

Christianity is not just a vertical relationship with God, but also a horizontal relationship with our fellow man. Ironically, when this vertical relationship and this horizontal relationship with each other intersect, it forms a cross. As I consider this picture, I realize that the cross of Jesus Christ is where *the justice of God* connects with *His grace* and flows out to us in a stream of mercy. In Philippians 2:5 the Apostle Paul reminds us to *"have the same attitude (or mind) as Jesus Christ,"* and that is an attitude of mercy that cries out against the injustice of this world. Yet, I must also realize that the cross is also the absolute statement of God's heart for justice. The reason that the Father sent Christ to die for us is because the justice He demands requires a price that you and I cannot pay. Jesus of Nazareth came and canceled the penalty and guilt of sin by giving His life in our place on the cross—the ultimate symbol of God's "Heart of Justice."

The denunciation of injustice and the cry for justice is loudest in the books of the Old Testament collectively referred to as the former prophets (Isaiah-Malachi). The collection of oracles that eventually came together to form the book of Isaiah begins with a denunciation of hypocritical worship. The people were going to the temple and performing all the required duties, but they were oppressing their neighbors. God says that He despises Israel's sacrifices and even hates their festivals because of their hypocrisy! God then says,

> *Learn to do good; Seek justice, Reprove the ruthless,*
>
> *Defend the orphan, Plead for the widow.*
>
> (ISAIAH 1:17)

Amos, a contemporary of Isaiah, utters the same disdain for hypocritical worship in the absence of justice. He said, as famously quoted by Martin Luther King, Jr.,

> *Let justice roll down like waters*
>
> *And righteousness like an ever-flowing stream.*
>
> (AMOS 5:24)

The prophet Micah pronounces the "Golden Rule of the Old Testament" when he says,

> *He has showed you, O man, what is good. And what does the LORD require of you? To act justly and to love mercy and to walk humbly with your God.*
>
> (MICAH 6:8 NIV)

What would these same prophets say if they walked into our worship services today? Are we attempting to worship God while ignoring the needs of the downtrodden? Are we helping to bring about justice in the world or are we contributing to injustice?

If God hates the shedding of innocent blood, and therefore injustice, then God desires for us to embody justice and live justly. But what exactly is justice? Justice is an abstract concept and therefore is often misunderstood. *Merriam-Webster's Dictionary* defines "justice" as "the quality of being just, impartial, or fair" and defines "just" as "acting or being in conformity with what is morally upright or good." In essence, justice means doing what is right, despite the consequences.

Every person has a built-in sense of justice. Even though it is often ignored, everybody has a basic sense of right and wrong. If you watch children play long enough, you will eventually hear one of them say, "Hey, that's not yours!" or "That's not fair!" We all have a built-in awareness of justice and injustice.

Where does this sense of right and wrong come from? In C.S. Lewis' classic *Mere Christianity*, Lewis uses this sense of justice as evidence for God (this is often referred to in apologetics as the "moral argument for the existence of God"). [5] Everybody at one time or another has said, "That's not fair." But what system are we appealing to? There must be some absolute, some standard of morality that we all intrinsically know. Lewis and others argue that our God imbues us with this sense of justice because He is a God of justice and He expects us to live justly.

Although we possess this sense of justice, true justice often slips through our fingers. Too often we confuse justice with what *we* think is fair for *us* at that moment. Often in our culture justice goes to the highest bidder. Singer/songwriter Derek Webb sings, "When justice is bought and sold just like weapons of war, the ones who always pay are the poorest of the poor."[6] Justice for the rich people and the poor people in the legal system of America is not the same. All too often the innocent are deprived of justice and criminals go free. It should not be this way in the family of God. He wants His people, His children, to uphold justice, to call for justice and to be the ones who live sharing His amazing justice with all the people we encounter in life. God warned the Israelites about this perversion of justice from the beginning when He said,

> *You shall not distort justice; you shall not be partial, and you shall not take a bribe, for a bribe blinds the eyes of the wise and perverts the words of the righteous.*
>
> (DEUTERONOMY 16:19)

Our sense of justice must be rooted in God and in His word. If our sense of justice is not rooted in God, it can easily become perverted. We may think that we are carrying out justice, when in fact we are just satisfying our own desires. Consider an extreme example, such as Adolf Hitler. Didn't Hitler think that he was acting justly? He believed he was actually within the will of God by trying to exterminate the Jews and was bringing true justice to the oppressed German people. However, this was perhaps one of the greatest acts of injustice in all of history! Therefore, we must check our sense of justice against God and His word.

Justice is one of God's essential attributes. He is a God that fixes the broken, puts the wrong to right. Jesus' healing of the blind, the lame, and the lepers foreshadowed how

God ultimately will make everything in creation right in the end. God's healing of the universe began when Jesus died on the cross. Through His death humankind was reconciled with the Creator. Now all of creation longs ultimately to be put right,

> *waiting eagerly for our adoption as sons.*
>
> (ROMANS 8:23)

How does God's desire for justice affect how we live? Just as God expected the Israelites to treat others with justice because they had been liberated from Egypt, He expects us to treat others with justice because He has liberated us from the bonds of sin. We are to convey to the rest of the world how God has reconciled all things in the heavens above and upon the earth below by dying on a cross and how one day everything will ultimately be put to rights.

> *For it was the Father's good pleasure for all the fullness to dwell in Him, and through Him to reconcile all things to Himself, having made peace through the blood of His cross.*
>
> (COLOSSIANS 1:19-20)

We must also remember that living justly does not mean that we only preach the Word. We are to take care of the physical needs of others and deliver justice to those who have been deprived of justice by the rest of the world as we communicate the gospel to them. It is hard to hear the gospel over the grumbling of an empty stomach or when one is dying of thirst or disease. God desires justice in His world and He desires for His people to be the ones carrying out justice in this world.

# CHAPTER THREE: AND JUSTICE FOR ALL
# 3 REVIEW

- What is the third thing God considers "an abomination" in Proverbs 6:16-19?

- What is the opposite of "hands that shed innocent blood"?

- Why does God tell Noah's family they are not to shed the blood of another human?

- What prompted God to free the Israelites from Egypt?

- Why did God have to constantly remind the Israelites that they were once slaves in Egypt?

- What is the relationship between loving God and loving others?

- What is the moral argument for the existence of God?

- How has God acted justly to His creation?

- What does it mean to "do" ministry both physically and spiritually?

- How can you bring about justice in the world around you?

# FOUR

## A HUNGER AND THIRST

The fourth item in the list of things in Proverbs 6 that breaks the heart of God is *"a heart that devises wicked plans"* (v. 18). According to ancient Hebraic thought, the heart was the seat of emotion (1 Samuel 2:1), desire (Psalm 37:4), and reason (Genesis 6:5). It wasn't until the time of the Greeks that the mind/brain became associated with reason. The heart represented the inner man; therefore, the heart could also be the seat of rebellion and pride. This is what the author of Proverbs 6:18 is addressing.

*A person who truly hungers and thirsts for righteousness does what is morally right, no matter what the consequences are.*

The author of Proverbs says that God hates a heart that devises *āwen*. This Hebrew word is often translated as "iniquity" or "misfortune." This is one of three primary words used for sin throughout the Old Testament. It usually refers to the work of those who walk in darkness in opposition to the righteous and the work of the righteous. Therefore, the antonym or opposite of a heart that devises *āwen* is a heart of righteousness. God desires for us to have a heart that hungers and thirsts for righteousness.

What exactly is righteousness? The term "righteous" is difficult to define. People often define "righteous" as being religious, but the meaning is much deeper and more far-reaching than that. It actually has a twofold meaning. First, it means loyalty and uprightness in a relationship, whether that is with man or with God (see Genesis 30:33). The second meaning is a legal term synonymous with "innocence." The Greek *dikaios* means "without prejudice or partiality of justice." W. E. Vine states that the term *righteousness* "embodies all that God expects of His people. The words, (to be right, to declare to be righteous, justification), associated with 'righteousness' indicate the practicality of this concept."[7] Both the Old and New Testament are abundant with the terms "righteous" and "righteousness" (it appears nearly 300 times in the Old Testament and over 200 times in the New Testament). If a concept occurs this many times, it must catch our attention! God definitely wants us to understand what this term means and apply the qualities of "innocence," "loyalty," and "uprightness" to our lives.

But what exactly does it mean to have a heart of righteousness? What does it mean to hunger and thirst for righteousness? A person who truly hungers and thirsts for righteousness does what is morally right, no matter what the consequences are. A person who truly longs for righteousness puts God first in all of his or her decisions. A person who truly desires righteousness puts others before himself or herself. A person who is truly righteous lives according to God's standards.

The prophet Ezekiel mentions three men whom he believed exemplified what it meant to be righteous. Noah, Daniel, and Job are men who conformed to God's standards (Ezekiel 14:14). They lived rightly in the sight of God, listening to and following His heart; this is righteousness. We must be alert to when Scripture directly characterizes a figure, understanding that God wants us to recognize a particular aspect of this person's character. Drawing attention in this way is rare and always has profound significance. If we want models for how to live righteously, these are three great men to turn to.

In the New Testament, Jesus praised those who seek righteousness when He said,

> *Blessed are those who hunger and thirst for righteousness for they shall be satisfied.*
>
> (MATTHEW 5:6)

Jesus doesn't say "they might be satisfied," or "they could be satisfied." Jesus states as a matter of fact that those who hunger and thirst "shall be satisfied!" What does it mean for that hunger and thirst to be satisfied?

In 1908 Sir Ernest Shackleton and three of his companions trekked across Antarctica to the South Pole. They were well equipped, but they underestimated what they would need for the perilous journey. Their return journey was a race against starvation. The explorers talked about what they would eat and what they would drink if they were able to sit at a great banquet table, at a great feast, or at one of their favorite restaurants. They were starving for just a tiny morsel of food. It was the promise and belief that if they completed their journey they would one day sit in a great restaurant and feast at a great banquet that drove them on and ultimately saved their lives.

In the same way, if we hunger and thirst for righteousness, that hunger will drive us on. Yet the reality of God's promise—that we will be satisfied, that we will have a seat at the greatest feast of all, at the Father's banquet table—is what sustains us. It really all comes down to what we are hungry for. What is it that you are hungry for? What is it that you are thirsty for? Many people in our culture desire the wrong things. Many people hunger for power and will do anything to exercise control over others. Others hunger and thirst for wealth and will do anything to get just one more dollar. Still others hunger and thirst for success. They want people to look at them and say, "Wow! Look at him/her." People in our world hunger and thirst for fame, beauty, popularity, security, riches—the list is long. However, what we should hunger and thirst for is righteousness.

In the Beatitudes, Jesus says that if we hunger and thirst for righteousness, our hunger and thirst *"shall be satisfied"*

(Matthew 5:6). Our hunger and thirst for righteousness leads to a deeper more meaningful relationship with Jesus Christ. He alone can ultimately satisfy our desire for righteousness; it is His desire to draw us close to Him, and it is that desire that allows us to approach righteousness.

Ironically, two of the terms that Jesus used to describe Himself relate to food and drink. In John 6:25-59, Jesus tells the crowds that He is the *"bread of life."* He tells them that regular bread will only leave them hungry. However, if they will *"eat of His flesh"* they will be truly satisfied. The story is very similar in John 4. Jesus is having a discussion with a Samaritan woman by a well, drawing water. The woman has come in the middle of the day to avoid the shame caused by her way of life as she is a woman the others speak of in hushed whispers. It is this woman Jesus asks for a drink of water. What is amazing is not that Jesus has asked for water but that He has spoken to her at all. I am quite sure this exchange has thrown her off balance; and before she realizes what is taking place, Jesus tells her that if she only knew who He was, she would have first asked Him for a drink. The woman understands only the reality of the physical world, not the spiritual life-changing truth Jesus has offered.

How could He give her a drink? He hasn't brought anything to draw water with? Jesus moves the conversation to where all truth is found, the spiritual, for the physical is temporary, the spiritual is eternal. Jesus explains to the woman that He is the *"living water."* If she continues to drink regular water, she will just become thirsty again; Jesus tells her that if she drinks of the living water, she will be satisfied. Our hunger and thirst for righteousness can only be fulfilled by the *"bread of life"* and the *"living water."*

Everybody has heard of the phrase "you are what you eat." That saying is definitely true when we talk about the *"bread of life"* and the *"living water."* As we feast and drink of Christ, we begin to look and act like Christ. One cannot come face to face with the Lord of the universe and not be changed by Him. As we seek after His righteousness, a little bit of His righteousness will surely rub off on us.

One of the questions we need to ask ourselves daily is "Am I truly driven by a hunger and thirst for righteousness? Do I truly crave the bread of life and the living water?" We don't come to church to nibble at the bread of life, scrape the crumbs off the table, or just smell the aroma. We come to be continually nourished by God and in some way become more like Him. We come to be filled with His goodness and absorb His righteousness.

Righteousness is simply doing the right thing for the right reason. Righteousness is trusting and obeying the One who gave His Son for you. We need to understand that God desires for us to hunger and thirst for righteousness. When we truly hunger and thirst for righteousness, we will be called "blessed" and will ultimately be satisfied. What are you hungry and thirsty for? Can you say that above all else you hunger and thirst for righteousness?

# 4 REVIEW

- What is the fourth thing God considers "an abomination" in Proverbs 6:16-19?

- What is the opposite of a "heart that devises wicked plans"?

- How would you define "righteousness"?

- Who are the three Old Testament characters specifically described as "righteous"?

- What does Jesus say about righteousness in the Beatitudes?

- What are some things people "hunger and thirst" for in your community?

- Do you think a hunger and thirst for righteousness is natural, or do you think it must be cultivated?

- How does Jesus fully satisfy our appetite?

# FIVE

# TRUE REPENTANCE

In previous chapters it was mentioned that the list of seven things that God hates begins at the eyes, literally "high eyes," and continues to move down the body to the "feet." The fourth thing that God hates and delineates in Proverbs 6:18 are *"feet that run rapidly to evil."*

*Which path are you taking? Are your feet running rapidly toward evil or are you running toward God, toward His open arms, as fast as you can? Repent, and come to God!*

In the classic poem "The Road Not Taken," Robert Frost describes two paths in the woods. He describes one path as being well trodden and worn and the other one as grassy and less worn. Frost then says:

> I shall be telling this with a sigh
>
> Somewhere ages and ages hence:
>
> two roads diverged in a wood, and I –
>
> I took the one less traveled by,
>
> And that has made all the difference. [8]

The Psalmist in Psalm 1 also tells of two possible paths. He says that one possible path is to *"walk in the counsel of the wicked."* This path clearly takes one away from God. The other path is walking toward God. If God hates feet that run rapidly *to* evil, then God must love feet that run swiftly *toward* Him. What must one do in order to run toward God? The journey starts with repentance.

The Scottish essayist and historian Thomas Carlyle understood the importance of repentance. He once said, "Of all acts of man, repentance is the most divine. The greatest of all faults is to be conscious of none."[9] Repentance is essential if one desires to run swiftly toward God. Unfortunately, many people think that repentance is merely feeling remorseful for something that they have done or feeling a sense of guilt.

However, neither of these are genuine repentance. True repentance is much deeper than that.

The Greek New Testament uses three different words that are variously translated, but all embrace the concept of repentance: *metánoia* (literally "to change the mind"), *apostrephō* (literally "to turn away"), and *epistréphō* (literally "to turn towards"). These three different meanings come together to form a good definition of repentance: A changing of the mind, a turning away from sin, and a turning toward God. It is not only a sense of guilt or shame, but it is a change of mind and active movement. This is exactly what the people did at Peter's Pentecost sermon. True repentance must include all three of these elements.

Why is changing of the mind essential for repentance? One must be willing to acknowledge that a sin is a sin before they can turn from it. If one attempts to stop committing sin but refuses to change his or her mind, he or she will just return to that same sin over and over again. There will be no real transformation. This is the reason why the first step in a twelve step program is admitting that you have a problem. Until you admit a problem, until you recognize that you have sinned, you cannot be healed.

For repentance to be genuine, it is essential to turn away from sin in order that you can then turn towards God. Our sins are against God's statutes, so it is only God who can forgive us. It is only through Him that we can have genuine repentance. New Testament scholar Robert H. Stein once put it like this: "One can only receive the grace of God with open hands, and to open those hands one must let go of all that would frustrate the reception of that grace."[10] One must be willing to let go of that which keeps us from coming to God. This is not an instantaneous process, but rather an ongoing process. We must to learn to crucify ourselves daily (Luke 9:23) and turn from our own sinfulness.

It is quite obvious that turning toward God is essential in order for repentance to be genuine. A right relationship with God is the goal of repentance, but this cannot happen if one does not run toward God. The change offered by a change of attitude without turning towards God is no different than the change offered by "self-help" books and day-time talk shows. This is not actual repentance. It is merely self-improvement.

Imagine for a moment that you are in a car somewhere in the Midwest, such as Kansas. You decide to make the long trek to Los Angeles. Now imagine after driving for a few hours you see a sign that says "Welcome to New York!" Obviously you have been going the wrong way for a long time! What must you do in order to get to Los Angeles? You have to do more than just recognize that you are going in the wrong direction. You would have to pull over, turn around, and drive back in the opposite direction. The same is true with repentance. It is more than just lamenting over your sins. It is feeling badly enough about them that you truly turn around and run back toward God. Just as in the illustration, there may be consequences for the sins we have committed and the backtracking may be arduous, but it is necessary if you want to get to your ultimate destination.

So what exactly would true repentance look like? A beautiful example of genuine repentance occurs in Acts 2. Fifty days after the death of Jesus, the holiday of Pentecost transpired. The early Christians were gathered together and praying when the Holy Spirit came down upon them. The Spirit enabled them miraculously to speak in tongues so that all of the foreigners in Jerusalem could understand them. A great crowd gathered to see what the excitement was all about. They thought the men were drunk! So Peter, the "front man" for the disciples, stood up and preached to the masses. His sermon is very powerful as he relates accusingly,

> *this Man . . . you nailed to a cross by the hands of*
> *godless men and put Him to death.*
>
> (ACTS 2:23)

As he preaches to the very Jews of Jerusalem who crucified Jesus, they are *"pierced to the heart"* (Acts 2:37) and ask Peter and the apostles what they must do to be saved. Peter responds by simply saying,

> *Repent and each of you be baptized in the name of*
> *Jesus Christ for the forgiveness of your sins.*
>
> (ACTS 2:38)

That day three thousand people repented, were baptized, and ran toward God.

Which path are you taking? Are your feet running rapidly toward evil or are you running toward God, toward His open arms, as fast as you can? Repent, and come to God! Turn back to your loving Father. When you take the path toward God, you will be able to say, like the poet Robert

74

Frost, that you chose the right path, and that it has made all the difference.

# REVIEW

- What is the fifth thing God considers "an abomination" in Proverbs 6:16-19?

- What is the opposite of "feet that run rapidly to evil"?

- What must one do in order to run toward God?

- What are the three elements of repentance?

- What is the difference between remorse and repentance?

- Do you have anything you need to repent of?

# SIX

# WALK IN INTEGRITY

The sixth thing that the author of Proverbs says that God hates is *"a false witness who utters lies"* (Proverbs 6:19a). This is similar to the second thing that God hates, *"a lying tongue,"* though there is a difference. The condemnation of a lying tongue seems to be a condemnation of lying in general, but the Hebrew phrase that is translated here as "false witness" implies an "injurious falsehood, in testimony, especially in courts."[11] Therefore, this is more of a legal term.

*Living with integrity is costly. Often those who have the most integrity suffer the most.*

Perjury in the ancient world was much more serious than perjury in our modern culture. From various Old Testament passages, it appears that an oath was considered an appeal to God to witness to the truth. Therefore, when one lied under oath, he not only wronged his neighbor, he also wronged God. He claimed that God was witness to the truthfulness of what was a false testimony. In our culture, if someone lies under oath they may be fined or possibly imprisoned, depending on the severity of the crime. However, if a person in Old Testament times was caught lying under oath, the punishment of the accused would be applied to him (Deuteronomy 19:16-19). Therefore, if one is caught lying about a crime worthy of capital punishment, the liar would be put to death.

Why would people bear false witness? Most often, it would be for personal gain or to avoid being punished for a crime. People lie to get ahead in life, despite the consequences. However, God wants just the opposite of that—integrity, honesty. In the Twenty-sixth Psalm, the psalmist condemns the deceitfulness of man, but goes on to say,

*"But as for me, I shall walk in my integrity"* (v. 11). This is what God desires of us: to walk in integrity.

What is integrity exactly? It is doing the right thing regardless of the cost. A beautiful expression of this occurred in the life of baseball legend Ted Williams. Every year, from 1939 to 1960, Ted Williams had a batting average well above .300, with the exception of one year. In 1959, Williams had a pinched nerve in his neck. He finished the season with a .254 average. He had a contract with the Boston Red Sox for $125,000, but he felt that he did not deserve such a large sum. He requested a thirty percent decrease to $90,000. He showed a tremendous amount of integrity when he asked for the pay decrease. How many athletes today do you think would do such a thing?

Integrity does not come naturally. Rather, it goes against the grain. God often requires us to live and act counter to our natural inclinations. Christianity in essence is countercultural; therefore, we must work at living lives characterized by integrity. Two great examples of people who continually sought for integrity in their day to day lives in the Bible are Daniel and Nehemiah. Both of these men were leaders for the people of Israel during times of adversity. Both of them had their integrity tested, but both stood firm.

In 605 B.C. the Babylonian Empire punished the small nation of Judah by taking 10,000 of the most gifted artisans, scholars, political and religious leaders, the most powerful people of Judah into exile into the land of Babylon (modern-day Iraq). Among this first deportation were Daniel and his three friends (later renamed Shadrach, Meshach, and Abednego). The king of Babylon, Nebuchadnezzar, attempted to force all of the Jews to follow Babylonian culture. However, many of the customs and tastes of their culture, such as the food, violated the Law of Moses. Daniel and his friends refused the special foods and rich dishes they were offered; they did what was right even though the situation was difficult and the demands were high. Daniel's integrity did not go unnoticed.

> *Daniel began distinguishing himself among the commissioners and satraps because he possessed an extraordinary spirit, and the king planned to appoint him over the entire kingdom.*
>
> (DANIEL 6:3)

Predictably, many of the Babylonian officials became jealous of Daniel's success. After all, he was a slave! He couldn't be appointed to rule over the kingdom! Therefore, they looked for a fault in him that they could report to the king, but

> *they could find no ground of accusation or evidence of corruption, inasmuch as he was faithful, and no negligence or corruption was to be found in him.*
>
> (DANIEL 6:4)

Daniel was a man of integrity.

Daniel did what God required of him despite his difficult circumstances. He was constant in his integrity. Whether he was in his homeland of Judah or in captivity in Babylon, he was faithful. He didn't just lean on God as a crutch when times were hard; he saw his vocation, not as a burden, but as an opportunity to demonstrate the truth, wisdom, and righteousness of the Living God. We also live in difficult times. We may feel like we have all types of things pulling us away from what God desires of us, just as the Babylonian culture was trying to pull Daniel and his friends away from God. Integrity calls us to be faithful in our vocation, to do right in times of ease and times of difficulty. God wants us to live with integrity so that we may be faithful witnesses to His truth.

Nehemiah's story takes place a century and a half later. The Babylonian Empire had fallen, only to be replaced by the Persian Empire, and the king of the Persians allowed the Jews to return home to their decimated land. Nehemiah returned from exile to serve as a governor for the small nation of Judah. When he arrived, he saw that there was no wall around the remains of Jerusalem. It had been totally destroyed by the Babylonians. Therefore, he set out to rebuild the wall.

Nehemiah did not desire to rebuild the wall to bring himself glory; he desired to rebuild the wall because it was part of his vocation as a governor. God had set him apart to serve the people. He was faithful in his duty and went above and beyond what was expected of him. He didn't just bring in forced labor to do his work; he was part of the building process. Perhaps Nehemiah's integrity shows through most when he says,

*I did not demand the governor's food allowance,*
*because the servitude was heavy on this people.*

(NEHEMIAH 5:18B)

He refused to live in luxury when his own people were suffering. Nehemiah was a politician who actually maintained integrity.

Why does God desire integrity in our lives? For one thing, the world desperately needs integrity. The Barna Group conducted a series of polls for non-Christians from the age of 16-29 years old and their view of Christianity. In these polls, the non-Christians showed that one of the things that they dislike most about Christianity is the fact that so many Christians are hypocritical and do not live up to what they profess.[12] These non-believers want to see a genuine Christian. They want to see someone who is characterized by integrity; they want to see someone who truly loves regardless of skin color, age, socio-economic, or political background. They want to see Christians *who actually look like Jesus.* We must reflect the character of God out into the world.

How does one go about becoming a man or woman of integrity? It does not just "come to us." It's not something that you can just pull off the top shelf and insert into your life. First and most importantly, honor and character is built by surrendering every aspect of your life to Jesus Christ and by immersing yourself in His Word. In order to learn the heart of God, we must spend time with God. Prayer, personal study, corporate study, and corporate worship are all essential for cultivating integrity.

Another thing that will affect our integrity is who we make friends with. There is a delicate balance in what Scripture teaches when it comes to this issue. On one hand, we are warned,

> *He who walks with wise men will be wise / But the companion of fools will suffer harm.*
>
> (PROVERBS 13:20)

On the other hand we have various stories of Jesus spending time with those whom the religious leaders had labeled "sinners." The question we must ask is, "Are we influencing our friends in a good way, or are our friends influencing us in a bad way?" We must preach the word to everyone, but we must not allow him or her to discredit or tarnish our integrity.

Living with integrity is costly. Often times those who have the most integrity suffer the most. There is no promise in Scripture that if you live uprightly, honorably, honestly then nothing bad will happen. Actually, Scripture teaches quite the opposite. Christ promises hardships and even persecution for those who truly follow the gospel.

So what do people see when they look at you? Would your co-workers say that you are an honest person? Would your friends say that you are characterized by integrity? God desires that we live lives marked by integrity. If we truly walk with integrity, we will make a difference in the world.

CHAPTER SIX: WALK IN INTEGRITY

# REVIEW

- What is the sixth thing God considers "an abomination" in Proverbs 6:16-19?

- Why was perjury a much worse crime in ancient Israel than it is today?

- What is the opposite of "a false witness who utters lies"?

- Who were the two biblical figures mentioned who were known for their integrity?

- What are some ways to cultivate integrity, honesty, truthfulness?

- Would people say that your life is characterized by integrity?

# SEVEN

# UNITED WE STAND

The final thing that God says that He despises in Proverbs 6:16-19 is *"one who spreads strife among brothers"* (v. 19b). In other words, God hates it when a person causes unnecessary division among people. Humans were

*Today there are thousands of denominations of Christians, but in the very beginning there was one united body, with one purpose.*

developed to live in community with one another. Division ruins this sense of community. Strife destroys friendships, marriages, families, and even churches. Therefore, if God hates strife and divisions, God desires unity for us.

If you read the creation story found at the beginning of the book of Genesis, you will notice that after every day of creation God evaluates His creation. Each time He declares that it is "good." This is repeated several times. However, in the second chapter of Genesis, God says something is "not good." This one thing that is not good is for man to be alone (Genesis 2:18). God had created Adam to rule over the beasts and tend the garden, but he was alone. Therefore, God provided him with a helpmate and eventually a family.

All people, in every culture, have a natural desire and need for community. N.T. Wright in *Simply Christian* suggests, "It seems that we humans were designed to find our purpose and meaning not simply in ourselves and our own inner lives, but in one another and in the shared meanings and purpose of a family, a street, a workplace, a community, a town, a nation." [13] Think of all the social relationships we have as humans: neighbors, co-workers, friends, spouses, relatives, clubs, teams, and committees. We were made for each other.

One of the ways that God has helped to satisfy that longing for oneness and community is the church. Today there are thousands of denominations of Christians, but in the very beginning there was one united body, with one purpose. Luke, the author of the book of Acts, summarizes the early life of the church:

> *They were continually devoting themselves to the apostles' teaching and to fellowship, to the breaking of bread and to prayer. Everyone kept feeling a sense of awe; and many wonders and signs were taking place through the apostles. And all those who had believed were together and had all things in common; and they began selling their property and possessions and were sharing them with all, as anyone might have need. Day by day continuing with one mind in the temple, and breaking bread from house to house, they were taking their meals together with gladness and sincerity of heart, praising God and having favor with all the people.*

*And the Lord was adding to their number day by day those who were being saved.*

(ACTS 2:42-47)

The early church made unity a priority. They devoted themselves to a type of fellowship which in the Greek is *koinonia*. *Koinonia* is a fellowship based on a deep affection or desire to share. The early church felt that fellowship with one another was essential for the life and growth of the church.

They also devoted themselves to the breaking of bread or communion. Communion serves a dual purpose: it brings a believer into communion with God and with fellow believers. The early church definitely believed this. A beautiful illustration of this is how the post-New Testament church shared the loaf of the Lord's Supper. When the church began to grow and multiple churches sprung up in cities, the churches wanted to maintain their sense of unity. Therefore, there would be one loaf of bread. The bishop of a congregation would break off a piece of bread for his congregation and then send the rest of the loaf to another congregation. This continued until every church in the community had a piece of the loaf.

Luke goes on to say that all the believers *"were together and had all things in common" (v.44).* In the early church, no one went without. If someone was rich and another poor, the rich person would sell what he had and give it to the poor person. This is exactly what Barnabas does in the book of Acts. He was a rich man who owned a valuable tract of land. Barnabas then sells this land and gives this money to the church.

What was the result of all of this unity?

> *The Lord was adding to their number day by day those who were being saved.*
>
> (ACTS 2:47)

When the church came together and was united, God used the church to accomplish His will. More and more people came to Christ. Is this really a surprise? Is it so shocking that when the outside world sees our love for one another they will want to join the church as well?

Of course, being united is much easier said than done.

So how can we work toward unity? First, we must learn how to be of the same mind. There is a difference between merely being together and being united. You can tie two people together who hate each other and they will be together, but they won't necessarily be united. Being united requires having the same shared goals and working together for those goals.

The church in Corinth was plagued with divisions. There seemed to be different factions who exalted one leader over another. One group claimed to be followers of Paul, others followers of Apollos, others followers of Peter, and some even claimed to be followers of Jesus alone. Therefore, one of the main issues Paul addresses in his first epistle to the Corinthians is their divisions. Paul becomes boldly sarcastic with the Corinthians and says,

> *Has Christ been divided? Paul was not crucified for you, was he? Or were you baptized in the name of Paul?*
>
> (1 CORINTHIANS 1:13)

Paul says to the Corinthians that his ultimate hope is

> *that you all agree and that there be no divisions among you, but that you be made complete in the same mind and in the same judgment.*

(1 CORINTHIANS 1:10)

Does this mean that everyone will perfectly agree on every theological concept? Absolutely not. If you were to bring together ten people who have studied the Bible, you would get ten different interpretations on certain passages. However, we must agree on core doctrines and we must have the same goal: love God and love others.

The church has been compared to both a river and a tree.[14] A river is composed of streams, melted ice, and other water sources. All of the water sources come together and flow as one, in one direction. A tree begins as a single seed or acorn of some kind and then grows into an enormous tree with huge branches. Like the river, the church is composed of people of all ethnic, cultural, national, and socio-economic backgrounds and comes together in one body. Diversity gives way to unity. However, the church is also like the tree.

We are all united in Christ, but we also express our faith and our gifts in a variety of ways. Unity gives way to diversity.

There is a difference between division and diversity. Diversity is a different way of expressing the same beliefs. For example, at Peachtree City Christian Church we have four services that are in three different formats. One is a traditional service that uses hymns and other traditional elements. One of the other services is our contemporary service. This service features an entire praise band with electric guitars and drums. Finally, our other two services are what we call "Café Worship." These services have more of a coffee shop feel and offer music and accompaniment by an acoustic band. This is an expression of diversity. We worship in different ways, but we have the same desires and the same goals. We all serve the risen Christ, we all hold the Lord's Supper as special and holy. We all are baptized into Christ in order to put on Christ, and we all heed the call to share the Good News in the world where we live.

Division, however, is destructive. Often times churches split over childish issues. Some churches have even split over the mere color of the carpet in the sanctuary!

Obviously, the color of the carpet is not a core issue but opinions, if not checked, can divide. We must be careful to make sure that we concentrate on the issues which unite us; that we are of the "same mind" as the Scriptures encourage us on the core issues of the Faith. As Thomas Campbell succinctly stated, "In essentials unity, in opinions liberty and in all things love."[15]

The second way we can have unity is to avoid selfishness or empty conceit. We live in a culture that elevates the self above all other things. Television and radio commercials and billboards constantly encourage our greed, our egos; they scream at us that we need more "things" in order to be truly fulfilled! These advertisements constantly tell us that we need to make ourselves skinnier, richer, happier, healthier, and prettier. We live in a world of ME-ism. However, it is impossible to have unity if we bring this selfish and conceited attitude into the church.

The Philippian church certainly had an ego problem. Philippi was a Roman colony. That meant that though they were outside of the city limits of Rome, the people of Philippi were treated like Roman citizens. They had tax-free status and were allowed to buy and sell property. Philippi was also like a retirement home for veterans of the Roman military. It is understandable why they would have such large egos. Paul, however, confronts this haughty attitude. He said,

> *Do nothing from selfishness or empty conceit, but*
> *with humility of mind regard one another as more*
> *important than yourselves.*
>
> (PHILIPPIANS 2:3)

Don't we often act just like the people of Philippi? Don't we too often think we are better than others and put ourselves before others? Common axioms in our culture such as "look out for number one" are evidence that we are trained to act selfishly. God, however, expects us to be humble. He expects us to see that we are no different than our brother or sister. We must understand that we are all in need of the grace and mercy of Jesus Christ. It doesn't matter how handsome you are, how wealthy you are, or how educated you are; everyone is in need of the grace and mercy of Jesus Christ.

I once heard a young man preach a sermon on unity in the church. Toward the end of his sermon, he asked a series of questions. He asked things like: Have you ever been lied to? Have you ever lost someone you love? Have you ever been hurt physically, emotionally, or in any other way? Have you ever wanted to give up? The young preacher went on and on with the questions. At the end of the questions, he said, "If any of these questions apply to you, please raise your hand now." Every hand in the room went up. He said, "Look around you. If Satan does not discriminate on the grounds of denominational background, skin color, wealth, education, or anything else, why do we?!" The young preacher makes a good point.

God desires for us to be united. We are His body and Christ's body is not divided. The best way we can be united is by making it a priority to regularly join our brothers and sisters in Christ in corporate worship. As we sing praises together to God, we are united. As we share in the breaking of the bread, we are united. As we listen to the Word of God being preached, we are united. As we give to help the church and to help others, we are united. God desires unity for us. If Christ was praying for our unity the night He was betrayed, it is certainly important enough for you and me to strive for unity in our lives.

# 7 CHAPTER SEVEN: UNITED WE STAND
# REVIEW

- What is the seventh thing God considers "an abomination" in Proverbs 6:16-19?

- What is the opposite of "one who spreads strife among brothers"?

- What was the one thing that God said was "not good" in the creation story?

- What kind of social relationships do you have in your life?

- What are some of the ways that the early church expressed its unity in Acts 2?

- What did Paul want the Corinthians to do to resolve the early church's divisions?

- What two images were evoked to describe the church?

- What is the difference between division and diversity?

- What did Paul want from the Philippian church in the passage discussed?

- Do you actively attend a church congregation?

# CONCLUSION

It has been a few years since I first developed the thoughts that have become the lessons of this book. As I write the conclusion for these seven chapters, some new thoughts concerning its pages even now come to mind. The first, and the most overwhelming idea, is that I continue to hold fast to the premise that I developed years ago on that beach as I watched my children play and as I contemplated the Word of God our Father.

Here is the premise that developed and that I continue to hold: God revealed to the writer of Proverbs these seven things that He wants us to stay away from, not so much in an effort to enforce His rules, but to direct our hearts. I believe that God wants His children to grow and that growth comes best when we are led to consider, contemplate, concentrate, and commit to the wisdom of His Word, His Truth. I still believe that God, as a Father, tells all His children the same truths, it's just that as we grow older, more mature, even wiser, we look with a deeper, more desiring gaze. Just as in the physical world, so too in the spiritual—the older we get the more we understand.

When I was three and my dad said, "Don't go in the street," all I was capable of understanding was "don't go" because my dad said so. When I was twelve I understood why he said it, and today I understand the love that inspired him to say it. So I hope that as you read this book the one thing that it does well is to help you consider, contemplate, concentrate and commit on a new, deeper level the love that inspired our Father to say, "Here are seven areas that I want you to take a closer look at—to examine carefully."

I believe that as we continue to mature, God our Father points us deeper and deeper into His Word, and He's not just concerned with pointing out the rules. One of the many things that I have come to realize is that our Father is not so much about enforcing the rules as He is about shaping hearts. Let's face it, if God wanted to enforce the rules, He has no problem taking care of the lawless; ask Sodom and Gomorrah. To me, the fact that there have not been more Sodom and Gomorrahs says that God our Father isn't as interested in enforcing the rules as He is in changing our hearts!

This book certainly does not exhaust this topic, it may not even come close, but I hope that it helps you to look a little deeper into the heart of His love, mercy, forgiveness and grace. I hope that it has encouraged you to think about the seven things God fervently desires for us; to see them again and again, and to recognize the heart of the Father who loves us so much that He sent His Son, Jesus of Nazareth, to ease the burden of the seven things He hates, so that you and I can focus joyfully on the seven things that He desires for us.

Finally, one of the most important things I hope you have gained from reading this book is that whenever you discover or discern something that God our Father asks us to stay away from or wishes for us to draw near to, it is vital that you remember this: There is one and only one motivating factor, His love.

# ENDNOTES

1 Thomas Aquinas, *Summa Theologica* (Question [163], Article [1]).

2 Joel, Billy. "Honesty." *52nd Street*. Columbia, 1978.

3 *Liar Liar*. Dir. Tom Shadyac. Universal Pictures, 1997.

4 Lathrop, Ann & Kathleen Foss. *Student Cheating and Plagiarism in the Internet Era: A Wakeup Call*. Englewood, Colo.: Libraries Unlimited, 2000.

5 C.S. Lewis. *Mere Christianity*. New York: MacMillan Publi. Co., 1952.

6 Derek Webb. "My Enemies Are Men Like Me." © 2005 Derek Webb Music (admin. by Music Services) All Rights Reserved. ASCAP. Used by permission.

7 W. E. Vine. *Vine's Complete Expository Dictionary of Old and New Testament Words*. Nashville: Thomas Nelson, Inc., 1996. 206.

8 Frost, Robert. "The Road Not Taken." *Literature Structure, Sound and Sense*. Laurence Perrin, ed., Atlanta. Harcourt, Brace, Jovanich, Inc., 1974. 627.

9 Carlyle, Thomas. Eminent English essayist, historian, biographer and philosopher (1795-1881)

[10] Robert H. Stein, *An Introduction to the Parables of Jesus*. Philadelphia: Westminster Press, 1981. 112.

[11] Brown, Francis, S.R. Driver, and Charles. Briggs. *The Brown-Driver-Briggs Hebrew and English Lexicon*. Peabody, MS: Hendrickson Publishers, 2004.

[12] Kinnaman, David and Gabe Lyons. *UnChristian: What a New Generation Really Thinks about Christianity . . . And Why It Matters*. Grand Rapids: Zondervan, 2007.

[13] Wright, N.T. *Simply Christian*. San Francisco: HarperCollins Publishers, 2006. 31.

[14] Wright, *Simply Christian*, 199-200.

[15] Campbell, Thomas. <u>Declaration and Address</u>. Washington, PA: 1809.

# ACKNOWLEDGEMENTS

There are many people who helped make this book possible and who without their willingness to serve and their gracious hearts it never would have been possible. I would like to thank them adequately but that is not possible, so I wish to express my thanks here so that you will know that this is not the work of one person, but the efforts of a family dedicated to the King of Kings.

First I have to thank Randall Cottrill who was the first person to suggest this book's creation. Then without Theresa Howard's hours of work in taking sermons and making them into written pages and Jeff Morgan's help in research and development it would never be understandable. To my good friend Joyce Revoir who believes in me more than she should and sees the big pictures better than most. To my editor and friend who brought it all together Lynn Horton, to Trisha Adams who is the creative designer, and of course, the Staff and Elders of Peachtree City Christian Church who encourage and support my ministry in every way. Thank you. I love you all.

George

# BIOGRAPHY

**Dr. George S. Dillard III** was born in 1958 in Jacksonville, Florida, while his dad served in the Navy. George is the oldest child of four brothers and one sister. In 1960 the family moved back to the Atlanta area where George would spend his childhood through college years. George calls Fairburn, Georgia, his childhood home. He graduated from Campbell High and from there went on to Atlanta Christian College. George grew up in the East Point Christian Church where he was ordained into the ministry in 1982. He graduated with a Bachelor of Science degree from Atlanta Christian College in 1983. In 1985 he answered the call of the First Christian Church in Rincon, Georgia, as his first full-time ministry. He received his Masters of Ministry in 1995 and Doctorate of Philosophy in Theology in 2001 from Evangelical Theological Seminary.

In 1993 George and his family moved to Peachtree City to answer the call of Peachtree City Christian Church where he continues to serve today. George has been happily married to his wife Renee for 21 years and have three children, Tiffany, Alexis and Stewart. George and his family live in Peachtree City, Georgia.

# ABOUT PEACHTREE CITY CHRISTIAN CHURCH

In 1972 a group of Christians came together to form a congregation in Peachtree City committed to Biblical preaching and following the pattern for the Church established in God's Word.

This group of people, seeking to be simply Christians, began meeting in the Peachtree City Elementary School. Soon they purchased three and a half acres on the corner of Wisdom Road and Riley Parkway and after a time constructed the first building. After many years of fruitful ministry in that location, the Church was led to relocate, purchasing 10 acres at the corner of Kedron Drive and Highway 74. After selling the Wisdom Road property, the congregation met at Kedron Elementary for 18 months while the current facility was under construction.

Today the congregation continues to commit herself to biblical truth and to being simply Christians. The church cooperates with many Christian missions in the local community and throughout the world to provide for the spiritual and physical needs of people. We see ourselves as not the only Christians but as Christians only.

We exist to Build Relationships, Introduce People to Jesus and to Grow Disciples. God has chosen to use His people in a mighty way here at Peachtree City Christian Church. We welcome the inquiries of all who would seek the will of God in any area of their lives.

For more information about our church and our ministries, visit our website www.PTCChristian.com.